Great Explorers

Captain Cook

by Jim Ollhoff

Visit us at
www.abdopublishing.com

Published by ABDO Publishing Company, PO Box 398166, Minneapolis, MN 55439.
Copyright ©2014 by Abdo Consulting Group, Inc. International copyrights reserved in all countries. No part of this book may be reproduced in any form without written permission from the publisher. ABDO & Daughters™ is a trademark and logo of ABDO Publishing Company.

Printed in the United States of America, North Mankato, Minnesota
052013
092013

 PRINTED ON RECYCLED PAPER

Editor: John Hamilton
Graphic Design: Sue Hamilton
Cover Design: Neil Klinepier
Cover Photos: Nathaniel Dance-Holland, Artist
Interior Photos & Illustrations: Getty-pgs 6, 7, 8, 10, 11, 13, 14 & 15; Glow Images-pgs 25 & 27; Herbert K. Kane-pgs 18-19, 21, 22-23 & 28-29; iStockphoto-compass illustration; John Hamilton-pgs 4, 12, 16 & 20; Library of Congress/Artist David Martin-pg 26; Princeton University Library-pgs 5, 17 & 18 (map); Thinkstock-pgs 9 & 24 & grunge map background illustration.

ABDO Booklinks
To learn more about Great Explorers, visit ABDO Publishing Company online. Web sites about Great Explorers are featured on our Book Links pages. These links are routinely monitored and updated to provide the most current information available. Web site: www.abdopublishing.com

Library of Congress Control Number: 2013931618

Cataloging-in-Publication Data

Ollhoff, Jim.
 Captain Cook / Jim Ollhoff.
  p. cm. -- (Great explorers)
 ISBN 978-1-61783-965-8
 1. Cook, James, 1728-1779--Travel--Juvenile literature. 2. Explorers--Great Britain--Biography--Juvenile literature. 3. Voyages around the world--Juvenile literature. I. Title.
 910.92--dc23
 [B]   2013931618

Contents

Unknown Lands

In the 1700s, Europeans didn't know much about the Pacific Ocean. They knew its approximate size because of Ferdinand Magellan's explorations in the early 1500s. They knew there were some fascinating and exotic unexplored places. There were hundreds of islands in the Pacific Ocean with undiscovered beauty and wealth. The vast markets of China and India held many opportunities. Europeans desperately wanted to trade with the people of the East, but getting there quickly and safely was a big problem. Most places were unmapped and uncharted. The Pacific Ocean was a vast unknown area.

Left: The exotic Na Pali Coast, on the island of Kauai, Hawaii. In 1778, Captain James Cook became the first European to make documented contact with the Hawaiian Islands. He named them the "Sandwich Islands" after John Montagu, the English Earl of Sandwich.

One of the great mysteries of the world at that time was a legendary continent called *Terra Australis Incognita*, which means "unknown land of the south." The ancient Greeks, during the time of Aristotle (384–322 BC) and Ptolemy (90–168 AD), knew the world was round. And they knew about all the land in Europe. But they believed that, because the Earth was perfectly balanced, the land at the top of the globe (Europe) had to be balanced by land at the bottom of the globe. So they believed there should be a huge continent on the bottom of the world. They called this imaginary land *Terra Australis Incognita*. In the 1500s and 1600s most mapmakers believed this land existed, and even drew it on their maps.

Below: An early 17th-century map of the legendary southern continent of *Terra Australis Incognita.*

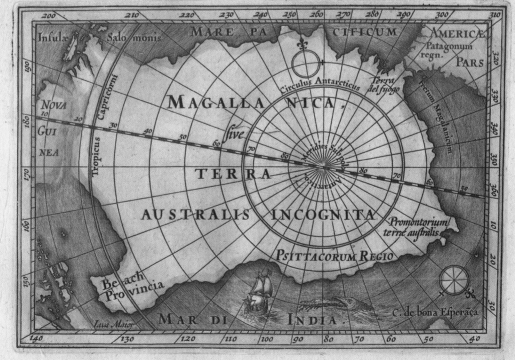

82 DESCRIPTIO TERRÆ SVBAVSTRALIS.

The explorations of Magellan proved that South America was not connected to this proposed southern continent. Other explorers had shown that Africa was also not connected. When Europeans discovered Australia, they thought it must be part of this southern continent. Whenever explorers discovered an island, they wondered if they had found *Terra Australis Incognita*.

Then along came Captain James Cook. One of Captain Cook's "discoveries" was to prove that there was no *Terra Australis Incognita*. Antarctica is a southern continent, but Cook realized that people could not live there. Captain Cook sailed around the Earth and charted and mapped huge areas of the world. He was one of history's greatest explorers.

Below: The *Endeavour*, a replica of one of Captain James Cook's ships, sets sail in Australian waters in 2011.

Captain James Cook said, "Ambition leads me not only farther than any other man has been before me, but as far as I think it possible for man to go." Cook sailed around the Earth and charted and mapped huge areas of the world.

Birth and Early Years

James Cook was born October 27, 1728, in the village of Marton, in Yorkshire, England. His parents were poor, so he had to go to work at an early age. In his teens he was an apprentice to ship owners. He became very comfortable on the ocean, and became an expert at charts and maps.

Right: Cook's seamanship training began in Whitby, along the coast of Yorkshire, England. Fishing remains an important industry in Whitby today.

In 1755, Cook joined England's naval forces, called the Royal Navy. He served during the Seven Years' War, where he further developed his talent for surveying and mapmaking.

Today, ship captains have many tools to guide their way. Satellite links and GPS systems tell sailors exactly where they are. Sonar and other technology can tell sailors the exact depth of the water. But in the 1700s, ship captains had no way to tell how deep the water was, or where exactly they were, unless they had a good map. If they had inaccurate maps, their ships could be wrecked by running aground or crashing into a reef. A good map was like gold to ship captains. And James Cook became one of the best mapmakers of his time.

Below: Satellite navigation systems on modern naval vessels would have astounded 18th-century sailors like James Cook, who often had to depend on inaccurate paper nautical charts.

1759–1767
The Mapmaker

Early in his Royal Navy career, James Cook charted the waters and lands of northern Canada. In 1759, he mapped the St. Lawrence River in Quebec. He married Elizabeth Batts (1742-1835?) in 1762, but soon was off to northern Canada again. By 1763, he was appointed to be an official mapmaker. He charted the lands and waters of Nova Scotia, Newfoundland, and Labrador.

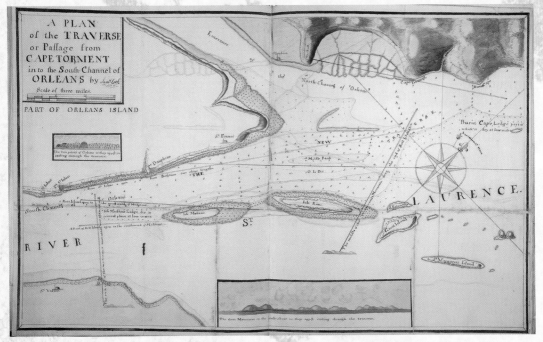

Above: Cook's talent as a mapmaker helped his Royal Navy career. This 1759 map of the St. Lawrence River near Quebec, Canada, highlights Cook's attention to detail.

Cook also began making a name for himself as a mathematician and astronomer. In 1767, he was promoted to the rank of lieutenant in the Royal Navy. In England in those days, it was rare for someone born to a poor family to rise through the ranks to a position of importance. But that's exactly what happened to James Cook. His skills as a navigator were so good, and his mapmaking was so accurate, that he was promoted again and again.

People liked sailing with Cook because he was humble and kind. He cared about his sailors, no matter what their rank.

Below: A humpback whale breaches near Witless Bay Ecological Reserve in Newfoundland, Canada. James Cook spent several summers surveying and mapping the craggy coast of this eastern Canadian island province.

First Voyage

In August 1768, Cook set sail with 94 sailors on the HMB *Endeavour*. It was mostly a scientific mission. They were to go to the South Pacific and watch the planet Venus move in front of the Sun. This was called the transit of Venus. They wanted to learn the speed at which Venus crossed the Sun. Then, they would be able to calculate more accurately the distance between the Earth and the Sun. Cook brought along an astronomer and other scientists, which was common for the time.

Below: A map of James Cook's first voyage from 1768-1771.

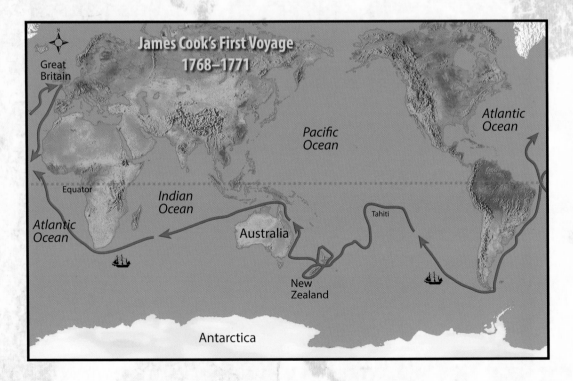

James Cook's First Voyage
1768–1771

Great Britain

Atlantic Ocean

Pacific Ocean

Atlantic Ocean

Equator

Indian Ocean

Atlantic Ocean

Australia

Tahiti

New Zealand

Antarctica

But there were secret orders, too. These orders were only made clear to the men of the *Endeavour* after they set sail. Their task was to search for the legendary southern continent of *Terra Australis Incognita*. English leaders were looking for another land to colonize, especially since the 13 colonies in North America were seeking independence at the time. The reason that Cook's orders were secret was that English politicians didn't want other countries to find out where Cook's ship was going. Sometimes, the explorers of new lands found gold, silver, spices, or other precious items. The English didn't want the Spanish, Dutch, French, or other rivals to find out what they were doing.

Below: A cutaway view of Cook's ship, the HMB *Endeavour.* The *Endeavour* was originally built in 1764 as a cargo ship. In 1768, it was purchased by England's Royal Navy for Cook's first expedition to the South Pacific.

HMB (His Majesty's Bark) *Endeavour*

Below: Tropical fish swim near a reef off the island of Tahiti. James Cook mapped the island and gathered information about the culture of the native people.

Cook sailed around the southern tip of South America, called Cape Horn, and then arrived in Tahiti in April 1769. Tahiti is an island east of Australia, now a part of French Polynesia. From Tahiti, they watched the transit of Venus. They spent several months on the island so that Cook could map it thoroughly.

They then sailed westward, reaching New Zealand in October 1769. They discovered that New Zealand was an island, and not part of the legendary southern continent.

Continuing to sail west, Cook mapped about 2,000 miles (3,219 km) of eastern Australia. It was the first time that Europeans had seen the eastern side of Australia. He claimed the land for England, and named it "New South Wales." At one point his ship ran aground on the Great Barrier Reef and was damaged. He landed in northern Australia to make repairs. The place he landed is now a city called Cooktown, named after the great explorer.

After making repairs to the *Endeavour*, Cook continued sailing north, mapping New Guinea and parts of Indonesia. Here, he lost about one-third of his crew to malaria, a disease carried by mosquitoes. Finally, in June 1771, Cook and his men arrived back in England.

Above: James Cook and men from the HMB *Endeavour* make first landfall in Australia at a place he called Botany Bay.

Second Voyage

Below: A map of James Cook's second voyage from 1772-1775.

During his first voyage to the Pacific Ocean, James Cook failed to discover *Terra Australis Incognita*. But English leaders still were not convinced that the legendary southern continent was a myth. They wanted Cook to continue searching, but this time they wanted him to go farther south. They gave him two ships, the *Resolution* and the *Adventure*.

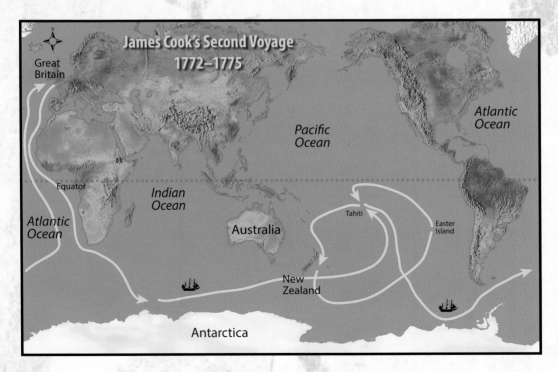

James Cook's Second Voyage
1772–1775

Great Britain

Atlantic Ocean

Pacific Ocean

Equator

Indian Ocean

Atlantic Ocean

Australia

Tahiti

Easter Island

New Zealand

Antarctica

Above: Cook's crew members collect chunks of icebergs for fresh water. In their ship *Resolution*, Cook and his crew were the first known people to cross the Antarctic Circle in January 1773.

Once again, Cook brought along scientists and artists. One of the crew members was a teenager named George Vancouver. Twenty years later, Vancouver would command a mapping exploration up the coast of northwestern North America. The Canadian city of Vancouver, British Columbia, is named after him.

The expedition left England on July 13, 1772. Cook sailed to the southernmost tip of Africa. This time, he went farther south. He became the first known person to cross the Antarctic Circle, a latitude close to the ice-covered continent of Antarctica.

Above: In 1773, Cook spent six weeks exploring and mapping New Zealand's Resolution Island and Dusky Bay (today's Dusky Sound). It became an important port for European ships.

The ships continued on to New Zealand, arriving in April 1773. They continued to explore and map many islands in the South Pacific. At one point, the *Resolution* and the *Adventure* became separated, and couldn't find each other. The *Adventure* eventually sailed back to England. Cook commanded the *Resolution* and continued its journey eastward. Cook stopped at Easter Island, Tonga, and the southern tip of South America. From there, the ship crossed the southern Atlantic Ocean. They found no legendary southern continent. They neared Antarctica during their journey, but had to turn back because of the cold. They crossed the Atlantic Ocean and ended up near the southern tip of Africa. They then sailed north. They arrived back to England in July 1775. Finally, English leaders were satisfied that the legendary southern continent of *Terra Australis Incognita* did not exist.

James Cook commanded the *Resolution*, using the ship to sail across both the Pacific and Atlantic Oceans.

Third Voyage

Below: A map of Captain Cook's third voyage from 1776-1779.

James Cook's second voyage proved to most people that *Terra Australis Incognita* did not exist. English leaders now had another question they wanted Cook to answer. Since before the time of Columbus, Europeans wanted a fast way to sail west to Asia. But, as European explorers discovered, North and South America were in the way. Ships from Europe that wanted to get to Asia or the South Pacific Islands from the east had to sail far south, to the southern tip of South America. It was a long, dangerous voyage.

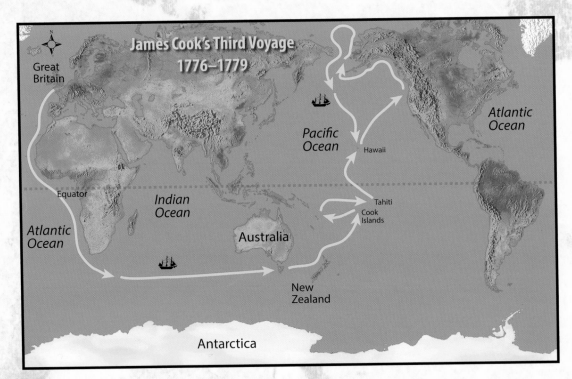

James Cook's Third Voyage 1776–1779

Great Britain

Pacific Ocean

Hawaii

Atlantic Ocean

Equator

Indian Ocean

Tahiti
Cook Islands

Atlantic Ocean

Australia

New Zealand

Antarctica

English leaders wanted to know if there was an undiscovered waterway across the northern part of North America. They called this legendary waterway the Northwest Passage. They had been looking for it on the eastern side of North America. But perhaps, they thought, it could more easily be found by exploring the western side of North America. They sent Cook to find the hidden waterway.

Now promoted to captain, James Cook sailed the *Resolution*, leaving England on July 12, 1776. His ship made it around the southern tip of Africa, then sailed eastward to Tahiti. Captain Cook loved the islands of the South Pacific.

In 1778, Cook sailed north and began mapping the Hawaiian Islands. He named them the Sandwich Islands after John Montagu, the Earl of Sandwich, who helped pay for Cook's expeditions. This was the same Earl of Sandwich who gained lasting fame for putting meat between two slices of bread.

Captain Cook sailed up the western coast of North America, all the way to present-day Alaska. He entered the Bering Strait, but the ice was too thick. He returned to Hawaii to wait out the winter and repair his ship. (Today, there actually is a Northwest Passage, but until recently it was always blocked by glaciers and ice. Cook's ship was only about 50 miles (80 km) from the entrance to the Northwest Passage.)

During this voyage, a change came over Captain Cook. The man who was perhaps the most careful mapmaker in history began to make navigation mistakes. His rules on the ship became more and more strange. When someone disobeyed the rules, his punishments were severe. The man who once cared about every sailor began to inflict horrible punishments and lashings on his own men. His punishments of the local islanders were even worse. He may have been suffering from dementia or depression, or perhaps was fatigued and burned out from years of ocean hardships.

In Hawaii, one of the islanders stole a small boat from the English sailors. Captain Cook attempted to kidnap the chief of the island to hold him ransom until the boat was returned. However, a skirmish erupted and Captain Cook was killed by an angry mob on February 14, 1779. His ship's crew returned to England on October 4, 1780, without their captain.

Cook's Legacy

A statue of Captain Cook in England.

Captain Cook was the greatest explorer of his time, perhaps of any time. He visited more places and covered more miles than anyone had ever done. He mapped thousands of miles of uncharted territory. His maps were very accurate. Some of his maps were used by sailors into the 1900s.

One of the most important contributions Cook made was the near-elimination of scurvy in his sailors. In those days, scurvy was a terrible disease that inflicted sailors on long ocean voyages. Scurvy victims suffered bone pain, swelling, bleeding, teeth falling out, paralysis, and finally death. Today, we know that scurvy happens when people don't get enough vitamin C. They didn't know about vitamins in those days, but Cook experimented with diets. He found that when sailors ate sauerkraut and citrus fruits (high in vitamin C), they didn't get scurvy.

Above: Sailors load citrus fruits aboard ship. Captain Cook's experimentation with diets helped him discover eating citrus nearly eliminated the disease scurvy.

For most of his career, Captain Cook seemed to be kind and humble. Perhaps he remembered his roots as a poor child, and wanted to treat others differently. While most European explorers tended to exploit those they encountered, Captain Cook was focused on mapmaking and exploring. For most of his time as an explorer, he conducted himself peacefully. Tragically, his personality changed on his last voyage, much to the dismay and horror of his crew.

During the Revolutionary War (1775–1783), the United States broke away from the rule of England. During much of this time, Captain Cook was exploring the South Pacific. The great American Benjamin Franklin wrote a letter to American naval commanders. Franklin said that if they were to meet Captain Cook's ship, they should not consider him an enemy. They shouldn't detain the crew or obstruct them, but rather help them in any way they could. Franklin said that they should treat "Captain Cook and his people with all civility and kindness, affording them, as common friends to mankind, all the assistance in your power which they may happen to stand in need of." Benjamin Franklin wrote that letter in March 1779, unaware that Captain Cook had died a month earlier.

Below: In March 1779, unaware that Captain Cook had died, Benjamin Franklin wrote a letter to American naval commanders stating that they should not consider England's Captain Cook an enemy.

Captain Cook was a skilled explorer, bravely mapping the unknown world.

Timeline

1728, October 27   James Cook is born in the village of Marton, in Yorkshire, England.

1755   Cook joins England's Royal Navy.

1759   Cook maps the St. Lawrence River in Quebec, Canada.

1762   Cook marries Elizabeth Batts.

1763   Cook charts the lands and waters of Nova Scotia, Newfoundland, and Labrador.

1767   Cook is promoted to the rank of lieutenant in the Royal Navy.

1768, August   Cook sets sail on his first voyage to see the transit of Venus and look for *Terra Australis Incognita*.

1771, June   Cook and his men return to England after their first voyage.

1772, July 13   Cook sets sail on his second voyage to look for the legendary southern continent.

1775, July   Cook returns from his second voyage. He is promoted to captain.

1776, July 12	Captain Cook leaves England on his third voyage, this time looking for the Northwest Passage.
1778, March-Oct	Captain Cook explores and maps the northwest coast of North America.
1779, February 14	Captain Cook is killed after a fight with Hawaiians.

Below: Captain Cook stands on the deck of his ship *Resolution* as Hawaiian King Kalaniopu'u is rowed out to the ship in Kealakekua Bay on January 26, 1779.

Glossary

Antarctic Circle

A latitude far to the south, close to the ice-covered continent of Antarctica.

Bering Strait

The waterway that divides Siberia, a vast area of central and eastern Russia, from Alaska. It was discovered by Vitus Bering in 1728.

Ferdinand Magellan

A Portuguese explorer who, in 1519, sailed from Spain looking for a way to Asia.

GPS (Global Positioning System)

A system of orbiting satellites that transmits information to GPS receivers on Earth. Using information from the satellites, receivers can calculate location, speed, and direction with great accuracy.

Great Barrier Reef

A system of coral reefs on the northeast coast of Australia.

Latitude

Imaginary lines that are drawn east and west around the Earth in parallel circles. Latitude is used to tell how far north or south one is from the Earth's Equator.

Navigator

A person in charge of plotting the direction of ships or other forms of transportation. Historically, navigators used the Sun and stars to find their way. As time passed, maps and special instruments were used. Today, many people navigate using GPS, the Global Positioning System, which uses orbiting satellites to pinpoint a location.

Northwest Passage

A legendary waterway between the Atlantic Ocean and Pacific Ocean.

Scurvy

A deadly disease, common among sailors at the time of James Cook, caused by a lack of vitamin C in the diet.

Seven Years' War

The Seven Years' War was fought from 1756-1763. Many European countries were involved. Great Britain and France were two of the major combatants. The armies of Prussia, Portugal, Austria, Russia, Spain, and Sweden also fought. Many of these countries, especially Great Britain and France, were long-time enemies. As their empires grew, their interests overlapped and caused conflicts. When war broke out, battles were fought in many places around the world, on land and at sea. By the time the long, bloody war ended in 1763, about one million people had been killed.

Sonar

A method of finding something submerged in water. A sonar device sends out sound waves and measures the time it takes for the echoes to return. The word comes from the phrase: sound navigation ranging.

Surveying

To measure the size, shape, and position of a body of land and/or water, often in order to create a map of a particular area.

Terra Australis Incognita

A land that people imagined would be in the southern Pacific Ocean. Captain Cook finally proved this imaginary land did not exist.

Transit of Venus

When the planet Venus travels between the Sun and the Earth, making it visible against the surface of the Sun.

Index